THE POCKET LIBRARY OF GREAT ART

Plate 1. AMEDEO MODIGLIANI
Photograph courtesy William S. Lieberman

AMEDEO

MODIGLIANI

(1884–1920)

text by
JACQUES LIPCHITZ

published by HARRY N. ABRAMS, INC., *in association*
with POCKET BOOKS, INC., *New York*

On the cover
detail of GIRL WITH BRAIDS *(plate 22)*

Plate 2. NUDE. *1917. Oil. The Solomon R. Guggenheim Museum, N. Y.*

Modigliani

For some strange reason, when I think of Modigliani
now, I always associate him with poetry. Is it because
it was the poet Max Jacob who introduced me to him?
Or is it because when Max introduced us—it was in
the Luxembourg Gardens in Paris, in 1913—Modigliani suddenly began to recite by heart the *Divine
Comedy* at the top of his voice?

I remember that, without understanding a word of
Italian, I was fascinated by his melodious outburst

and his handsome appearance: he looked aristocratic even in his worn-out corduroys. But even after I had known him a long time, Modigliani would surprise us often with his love and knowledge of poetry— sometimes at the most awkward moments.

I recall a scene, one night (it must have been in 1917) very late, maybe three o'clock in the morning. We were suddenly aroused from our sleep by a terrific pounding on the door. I opened. It was Modigliani, obviously quite drunk. In a shaky voice he tried to tell me he remembered seeing on my shelf a volume of poetry by François Villon and he said he would like to have it. I lighted my kerosene lamp to find the book, hoping that he would leave so that I could go back to sleep. But no; he settled down in an armchair and began to recite in a loud voice.

I was living at that time at 54 rue du Montparnasse in a house occupied by working people, and soon my neighbors began to knock on the walls, on the ceiling, on the floor of my room, shouting, "Stop that noise!" This scene is still vivid in my mind: the small room, the darkness of the middle of the night interrupted only by the flickering, mysterious light of the kerosene lamp, Modigliani, drunk, sitting like a phantom in the armchair, completely undisturbed, reciting Villon, his voice growing louder and louder, accompanied by an orchestra of knocking sounds from all around our little cell. Not until he exhausted himself, hours later, did he stop.

We often discussed poetry—Baudelaire, Mallarmé,

Plate 3. THE BEGGAR OF LEGHORN. *1909. Oil*
Collection Dr. Paul Alexandre, Paris

Rimbaud—and more often than not he would recite by heart some of their verses. His love for poetry touched me, but I admired even more his obviously remarkable memory.

But now, when I think back to the time when I first met Modigliani, in the Luxembourg Gardens, I cannot dissociate that glorious scene—the Parisian sunshine, the beautiful greenness around us—from the tragic end of Max Jacob, marvelous poet and delicate friend. When I heard about Max's sufferings in the concentration camp of Drancy early in the German occupation of France, when I read about him lying among other martyrs on the dirty floor, dying slowly and painfully, immediately the scene in the Luxembourg Gardens came vividly to mind.

The *Divine Comedy* recited by Modigliani and the hell suffered by Max Jacob together make a pathetic image worthy of Modigliani's memory. He knew what it was to suffer, too. He was sick with tuberculosis which killed him; he was hungry and poor. But he was at the same time a *riche nature*—so lovable, so gifted with talent, with sensitivity, with intelligence, with courage. And he was generous—promiscuous, even—with his gifts, which he scattered recklessly to the winds in all the hells and all the artificial paradises.

Before I was introduced to him, I had frequently seen Modigliani in cafés and on the streets of Montparnasse. A friend of mine, Cesare Sofianopulo, painter and poet from Trieste who was one of my

Plate 4. DR. PAUL ALEXANDRE. *1911. Oil*
Collection Dr. Paul Alexandre, Paris

fellow students at the Académie Julian in 1911 and whose portrait I made at this time, reminded me in a letter just before the Second World War that Modigliani went to school with us, too. I don't remember that at all. The first time we met was when Max Jacob introduced me to him, and Modigliani invited me to his studio at the Cité Falguière. At that time he was making sculpture, and of course I was especially interested to see what he was doing.

When I came to his studio—it was spring or summer—I found him working outdoors. A few heads in stone—maybe five—were standing on the cement floor of the court in front of the studio. He was adjusting them one to the other.

I see him as if it were today, stooping over those heads, while he explained to me that he had conceived all of them as an ensemble. It seems to me that these heads were exhibited later the same year in the Salon d'Automne, arranged in stepwise fashion like tubes of an organ to produce the special music he wanted.

Modigliani, like some others at the time, was very taken with the notion that sculpture was sick, that it had become very sick with Rodin and his influence. There was too much modeling in clay, "too much mud." The only way to save sculpture was to start carving again, direct carving in stone. We had many very heated discussions about this, for I did not for one moment believe that sculpture was sick, nor did I believe that direct carving was by itself a solution to anything. But Modigliani could not be budged; he

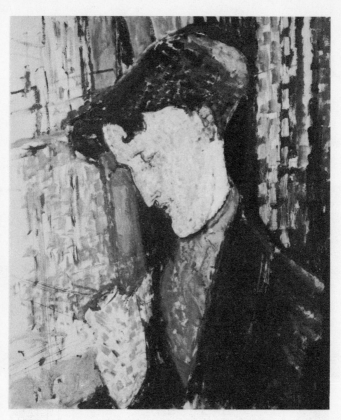

Plate 5. FRANK BURTY HAVILAND. *About 1914. Oil*
  Collection Gianni Mattioli, Milan

Plate 6. HEAD. *1914-15. Limestone*
The Museum of Modern Art, New York

Plate 7. HEAD. *1915. Limestone*
Collection Mrs. Orswell Dailey, Pomfret, Conn.

Plate 8. CARYATID. *About 1914. Limestone*
The Museum of Modern Art, New York

Plate 9. ROSE CARYATID. *About 1914. Gouache, pencil, and crayon*
Norton Gallery and School of Art, West Palm Beach, Florida

Plate 10. BEATRICE HASTINGS. *About 1915. Pencil and crayon*
The Solomon R. Guggenheim Museum, New York

held firmly to his deep conviction. He had been seeing a good deal of Brancusi, who lived nearby, and he had come under his influence. When we talked of different kinds of stone—hard stones and soft stones—Modigliani said that the stone itself made very little difference; the important thing was to give the carved stone the feeling of hardness, and that came from within the sculptor himself: regardless of what stone they use, some sculptors make their work look soft, but others can use even the softest of stones and give their sculpture hardness. Indeed, his own sculpture shows how he used this idea.

It was characteristic of Modigliani to talk like this. His own art was an art of personal feeling. He worked furiously, dashing off drawing after drawing without stopping to correct or ponder. He worked, it seemed, entirely by instinct—which, however, was extremely fine and sensitive, perhaps owing much to his Italian inheritance and his love of the painting of the early Renaissance masters. He could never forget his interest in people, and he painted them, so to say, with abandon, urged on by the intensity of his feeling and vision. This is why Modigliani, though he admired African Negro and other primitive arts as much as any of us, was never profoundly influenced by them—any more than he was by Cubism. He took from them certain stylistic traits, but he was hardly affected by their spirit. His was an immediate satisfaction in their strange and novel forms. But he could not permit abstraction to interfere with feeling, to get between him and his subjects. And that is why his portraits are such remarkable characterizations and why his nudes are so sexually frank. Incidentally, I would like to mention two other artists whose work influenced Modigliani's style, and who are not often mentioned in this connection: Toulouse-Lautrec and —Boldini, who years ago enjoyed the reputation of being one of Europe's most prominent and most fashionable society portraitists.

If Modigliani's convictions were strong, so were

Plate 11. MAUD ABRANTES WRITING IN BED. *1908. Pencil*
Collection Dr. Paul Alexandre, Paris

COLOR PLATE *(12)*. THE CELLIST *(study)*. *1909*
Oil, 29 x 23½". Collection Dr. Paul Alexandre, Paris

also his pride and his courage, which bordered almost on recklessness. I want to recall here one well-known incident which illuminates these traits in his character. Modigliani was not a physically strong man, yet one day in a café he attacked all by himself a gang of royalists, who in France are known for their soldierly courage. He wanted to fight them because he had heard them speaking against the Jews in a dirty way. Modigliani was naturally conscious of his Jewishness and could not bear any unfair criticism of a whole people. He was not urged on by political or

Plate 13
FIGURE
*1914-15. Limestone
Curt Valentin Gallery
New York*

COLOR PLATE *(14)*. CARYATID. *1912. Oil, 32¼ x 18"*
Collection Avv. Verdirame, Milan

other motives; it was just an inborn part of his personality. This was a very characteristic trend of his nature, understandable because he came from a very old Italian-Jewish family. His mother was a descendant of the great philosopher Spinoza; I heard him speak often about his mother, whom he adored and respected.

His judgment of the plastic arts was very good. It

Plate 15. "MADAM POMPADOUR." 1915. Oil
The Art Institute of Chicago (Winterbotham Coll.)

COLOR PLATE *(16)*. FAT CHILD. *1915. Oil, 18½ x 15"*
Private collection, Milan

Plate 17. KISLING. *1916. Crayon*
Collection Mr. and Mrs. Ira Herbert, New York

was he who helped Chaim Soutine, the painter, who
at that time was known to only a few of us. And it
was also he who induced Leopold Zborowski, his own
dealer, to take an interest in Soutine's painting.
Shortly before his death, a very sick man, Modigliani
said to Zborowski, "Don't worry, in Soutine I am
leaving you a man of genius." To understand this
sentence better, one has to know more about the relationship between Modigliani and his dealer.

Leopold Zborowski, a Polish poet, poor but with a

COLOR PLATE *(18)*. KISLING. *1915*. *Oil, 14½ x 10¾"*
Collection Jesi, Milan

great love for art, was trying hard to make a living in the hungry Montparnasse at the beginning of the First World War. He bought and sold books, and with the little he made on those operations he acquired paintings—first from his neighbor and friend, Kisling, and later, on Kisling's advice, he began to deal with Modigliani. Kisling was always a very good friend to Modigliani. I saw Modigliani frequently working in Kisling's studio, using the latter's models

Plate 19. BEATRICE HASTINGS. *1916.* Oil
Private collection, U. S.

COLOR PLATE (20). PAUL GUILLAUME. 1916. Oil, 31½ x 21¼"

Museum of Modern Art, Milan

and also his materials, and meeting the many people who came to see Kisling, a warm and generous comrade.

Little by little Zborowski became successful with his painters; he became known as the dealer of Modigliani, whose work in later years turned out to be a good source of income for him. That is why Modigliani, feeling his untimely end approaching, told Zborowski not to worry since he was leaving him Chaim Soutine, a painter of genius.

The connection between Modigliani and Zborow-

Plate 21
NUDE WOMAN
1917. Pen and was.
Coll. Jacques Sarli
New York

COLOR PLATE (22). GIRL WITH BRAIDS (THE PINK BLOUSE). 1917
Oil, 23½ x 17½". Collection Mrs. Sam A. Lewisohn, New York

ski is a remarkable example of the almost family relationship that existed between many artists and their dealers at that time in Paris. Not all the dealers were exploiters and slave drivers. And the same was true for some collectors who were not thinking at all about investments when they bought a painting or sculpture. Some were real art lovers, like the charming M. Dutilleul whose portrait was done beautifully by Modigliani, or Alphonse Kann who was trembling when he came to see my studio. So attracted was he when he discovered some new sculptures which he had not seen before that he would not leave my studio without taking them with him to his wonderful home. And there were many more like these two, with a genuine love for art.

In 1916, having just signed a contract with Léonce Rosenberg, the dealer, I had a little money. I was also newly married, and my wife and I decided to ask Modigliani to make our portrait (plates 45 & 46). "My price is ten francs a sitting and a little alcohol, you know," he replied when I asked him to do it. He came the next day and made a lot of preliminary drawings, one right after the other, with tremendous speed and precision, as I have already stated. Two of these drawings, one of my wife and one of myself, are reproduced in this book (plates 44 & 54). Finally a pose was decided upon—a pose inspired by our wedding photograph.

The following day at one o'clock, Modigliani came with an old canvas and his box of painting materials,

COLOR PLATES *(23 & 24)*. BRIDE AND GROOM. *1915*
Oil, 23¼ x 18¼″. The Museum of Modern Art, New York

ENTIRE PAINTING ABOVE
◄— LIFT FOLD FOR DETAIL

and we began to pose. I see him so clearly even now—
sitting in front of his canvas which he had put on a
chair, working quietly, interrupting only now and
then to take a gulp of alcohol from the bottle standing nearby. From time to time he would get up and
glance critically over his work and look at his models.
By the end of the day he said, "Well, I guess it's finished." We looked at our double portrait which, in
effect, was finished. But then I felt some scruples at
having the painting at the modest price of ten francs;

Plate 25. LEOPOLD ZBOROWSKI. *1917*. *Pencil*
Museum of Art, Rhode Island School of Design, Providence

COLOR PLATE (26). LEOPOLD ZBOROWSKI. 1917. Oil, 42 x 26"

Museu de Arte, São Paulo, Brazil

it had not occurred to me that he could do two portraits on one canvas in a single session. So I asked him if he could not continue to work a bit more on the canvas, inventing excuses for additional sittings. "You know," I said, "we sculptors like more substance." "Well," he answered, "if you want me to spoil it, I can continue."

As I recall it, it took him almost two weeks to finish our portrait, probably the longest time he ever devoted to working on one painting.

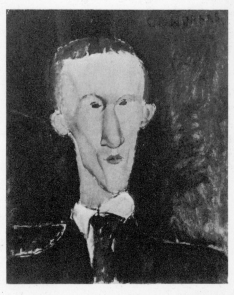

Plate 27. BLAISE CENDRARS. *1917. Oil*
Private collection, Connecticut

COLOR PLATE *(28)*. DR. DEVARAIGNE. *1917. Oil, 21¾ x 18"*
Collection Mrs. John W. Garrett, Baltimore

This portrait had been hanging on my wall for a long time until one day I wanted my dealer to return to me some sculptures in stone which I no longer felt were representative. He asked me more money than I could afford, and the only thing I could do was to offer as an exchange the portrait by Modigliani—who by that time was already dead. My dealer accepted, and as soon as I had my stones back I destroyed them. And that's how it happens that this portrait came

Plate 29
CHAIM SOUTINE
1918. Oil
Private collection
Paris

COLOR PLATE (*30*). JEAN COCTEAU. *1917. Oil, 39½ x 32"*
Collection Henry Pearlman, New York

finally to be in the collection of The Art Institute of Chicago.

It was two years later, in 1922, that the great American collector, Dr. Albert C. Barnes, discovered Modigliani as well as Soutine. (A year or so ago I was saddened to learn of the frightful death of this remarkable man, in an automobile accident.) In the apartment of Zborowski, 3 rue Joseph-Bara, Dr. Barnes bought a great many of their paintings. I remember the day very well, this day which caused a lot of noise on Montparnasse and will remain forever

COLOR PLATE *(32)*. PORTRAIT OF MARGUERITE. *1917. 18 x 20"*
Collection Mr. and Mrs. Harry N. Abrams, New York

in the annals of art history. It was at this point that the two friends, Modigliani and Soutine, began to win international recognition. It was very appropriate for the Cleveland Museum of Art to reunite them in 1951 in a splendid joint exhibition.

In the last years of his life Modigliani became increasingly devoted to Soutine, who had only a small studio but was always ready to share what he had with his friend. Modigliani's health was now completely undermined, his fits of coughing kept him from getting rest, and he drank more and more. Zborowski had scraped together some money to send him to Nice during the winter of 1919 for his health, but this did not help him. He was living at this time with Jeanne Hebuterne and their little girl in a small apartment. Little by little Modigliani's pictures were beginning to be sold, and we all hoped that a more ordered existence and better luck might yet be his. And then, in January of 1920, Kisling brought us the shocking news of his death.

Modigliani had been taken to the hospital one day, and the next day he was gone. We were told that on the way to the hospital he kept repeating *"Italia! Cara Italia!"* and that in his last moments of consciousness he fought wildly to hold on to life, babbling verses in his delirium.

And then came the tragic news of Jeanne Hebuterne's suicide. She was about nine months pregnant with another child by Modigliani, and when she arrived at the hospital morgue, she threw herself upon

LIFT FOLD FOR ENTIRE PAINTING ⟶
DETAIL AT RIGHT

Modigliani and covered his face with kisses. She fought with the officials who pulled her away because they knew how dangerous it was for her—pregnant as she was—to touch the open sores that covered his face. She was a strange girl, slender, with a long oval face which seemed almost white rather than flesh color, and her blond hair was fixed in long braids; she always struck me as looking very Gothic. Jeanne Hebuterne went to her father's house—she had been disowned for living with Modigliani—and she threw

Plate 35
BOY WITH RED HAIR
About 1919. Oil
Coll. Ralph M. Coe
Cleveland

COLOR PLATE *(36)*. YOUNG GIRL WITH BROWN HAIR. *1918*
Oil, 26 x 18". Collection Jesi, Milan

Plate 37. GIRL IN CHEMISE (LA PETITE LAITIERE)
1918. Oil. Paul Rosenberg & Co., New York

herself from its rooftop. Her family forbade that she
be buried beside Modigliani, but I believe they were
afterwards brought together.

Looking at his handsome likeness it is not difficult
to understand that women were so crazy about him:
Beatrice Hastings, Jeanne Hebuterne, and others
whose names we did not even know—including the
little student girl who died of tuberculosis not long
after Modigliani's death.

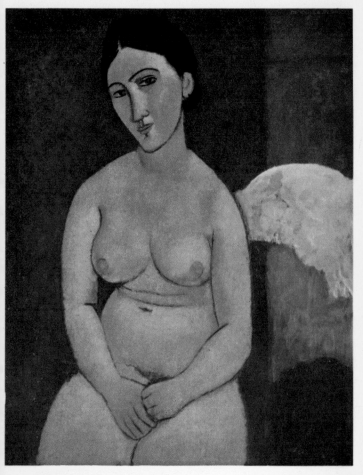

COLOR PLATE *(38)*. SEATED NUDE. *1918. Oil, 32½ x 26⅜"*
Collection Mr. and Mrs. Leigh B. Block, Chicago

I will never forget Modigliani's funeral. So many friends, so many flowers, the sidewalks crowded with people bowing their heads in grief and respect. Everyone felt deeply that Montparnasse had lost something precious, something very essential.

Kisling and Moricand, a friend, tried to make Modigliani's death mask. But they did it very badly and came to me for help with a lot of broken pieces of plaster full of adhering bits of skin and hair. Patiently, I put the fragments together, and since many

Plate 39. LUNIA CZECHOWSKA (THE WHITE BLOUSE). *1917-18. Oil Collection Mr. and Mrs. Sydney M. Shoenberg, Jr., St. Louis*

COLOR PLATE (40). LUNIA CZECHOWSKA. 1919. Oil, 18½ x 13"
Collection Carlo Frua de Angeli, Milan

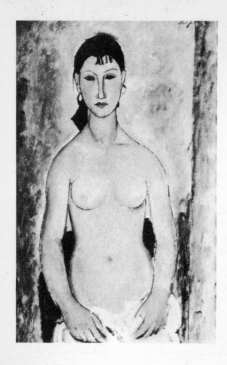

Plate 41
ELVIRA
1919. Oil
Private collection
Switzerland

pieces were missing, I had to restore these missing parts as well as I could. Altogether I made twelve plaster molds, which were distributed among Modigliani's family and friends.

When he died, Modigliani was far from being unknown. Paris was filled with strange and striking people, many with talent and some with genius, but he always stood out. And among us his reputation as a painter was established, although, as I have said, it was not until 1922, when Dr. Barnes discovered

LIFT FOLD FOR ENTIRE PAINTING →
DETAIL AT RIGHT

Plate 44. BERTHE LIPCHITZ. *1916. Pencil*
Collection Jacques Lipchitz, New York

his work, that he began to be known internationally.

Up to that time Zborowski had worked hard and faced many difficulties in bringing his friend's work to the public. I remember two shows which Zborowski arranged in 1915 or '16. One of them was in a small store near the Tuileries, and in it were several portraits of Zborowski done with the heavy impasto which Modigliani later abandoned. But Zborowski's most ambitious attempt during Modigliani's lifetime was a show he arranged in 1917 at the Berthe Weill

ENTIRE PAINTING AT RIGHT
LIFT FOLD FOR DETAIL ➞

COLOR PLATES (*45 & 46*). JACQUES LIPCHITZ AND HIS WIFE. *1916-17*
Oil, 31½ x 21". The Art Institute of Chicago

gallery in the rue Laffitte. To catch the eye of the
public he had placed in the window four of Modigliani's nudes. Unfortunately it was the police who
saw them first, and they made Zborowski take them
out of the window. He came to me heartbroken. He
had placed all his hopes in that show and now he was
afraid that there would be nothing to draw people off
the street into the gallery. He offered to sell the four
nudes to me for five hundred francs, but what could
I do with four nudes on my walls?

Plate 47. GYPSY WOMAN WITH BABY. *1919. Oil*
National Gallery of Art, Washington, D. C.
(Chester Dale Collection, Loan)

COLOR PLATE *(48)*. JEANNE HEBUTERNE. *1919. Oil, 51 x 32"*
Collection Mr. and Mrs. Sidney F. Brody, Beverly Hills, Calif.

Plate 49. GIRL IN THE WHITE BLOUSE. *1918. Oil*
Collection Walter Maitland, Drake, Colorado

Some years later a nude by Modigliani—perhaps
one of the four—was bought for close to a million
francs by a French collector. Within a few years after
his death Modigliani's paintings were eagerly sought
for and collected, and their value is still increasing.

Compared with the life of a Titian or a Michel-
angelo, Modigliani's life was a brief flash of brilliance.
Would he have painted as well if he had lived a different kind of life, less dissipated and more disci-
plined? I do not know. He was aware of his gifts, but
the way he lived was in no way an accident. It was

COLOR PLATE (50). ELVIRA. 1919. Oil. 36 x 23¼"
Collection Mr. and Mrs. Joseph Pulitzer, Jr., St. Louis

his choice. One night during dinner I saw how ill he looked. He was eating in a strange way, almost covering his food with salt and pepper before even tasting it. But when I began to urge him to be less self-destructive and to put some kind of order into his life, he became as angry as I had ever seen him.

As I come to the end of this brief account I would like to say that although Modigliani died so young, he accomplished what he had always wanted. He said to me time and again that he wanted a short but intense life—*"une vie brève mais intense."*

Plate 51. PORTRAIT OF MARIO. *1920. Oil*
Collection Mr. and Mrs. Francisco M. Sobrinho
São Paulo, Brazil

COLOR PLATE (52). SELF-PORTRAIT. 1919. Oil, 33½ x 23½"
Collection Mr. and Mrs. Francisco M. Sobrinho, São Paulo, Brazil

Plate 53. ROSA PORPRINA. *1915. Colored pencil and oil*
Collection Dr. Riccardo Jucker, Milan

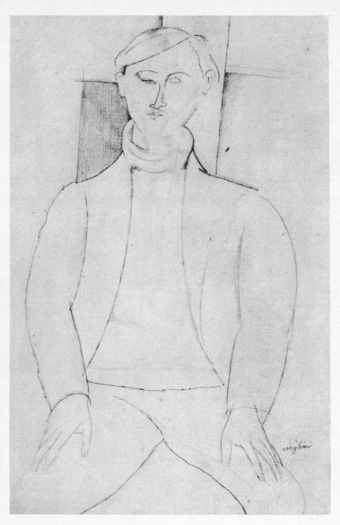

Plate 54. JACQUES LIPCHITZ. *1916. Pencil*
Collection Jacques Lipchitz, New York

Plate 55. CHARLES-ALBERT CINGRIA. *About 1918*
Ink and pencil. Brooklyn Museum, New York

Plate 56. PORTRAIT OF A WOMAN. *1919. Pencil*
The Museum of Modern Art, New York

Plate 57. ANNA ZBOROWSKA. *1917. Pencil*
Museum of Art, Rhode Island School of Design, Providence

Plate 58. ANNA ZBOROWSKA. *1917. Oil*
The Museum of Modern Art, New York (Lillie P. Bliss Coll.)

Plate 59. LEON BAKST. *About 1915. Oil*
National Gallery of Art, Washington, D. C.
(Chester Dale Collection, Loan)

Plate 60. JUAN GRIS. *1916. Oil*

Collection Miss Adelaide Milton de Groot, New York

Plate 61. RECLINING NUDE. *1919. Oil. Formerly collection Paul Gu*

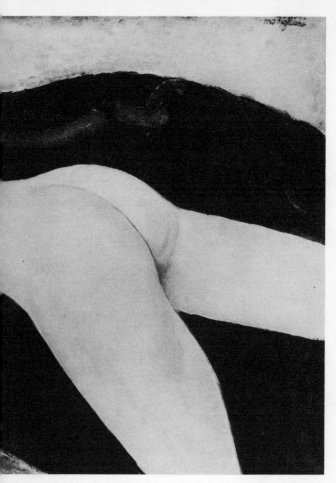

Paris

Plate 62. TWO TREES, CAGNES. *1918. Oil*
Formerly collection Paul Guillaume, Paris

Plate 63. HOUSE AT CAGNES. *1918. Oil*
Private collection, Paris

Plate 64. SEATED BOY. *1918. Oil*
Formerly collection Paul Guillaume, Paris

BIOGRAPHICAL NOTES

1884   Amedeo Modigliani (pronounced *moe-deel-YAHN-ee*) born July 12, Leghorn, Italy.

1898   Illness interrupts formal schooling; begins painting, instructed by local artist Micheli.

1900–02   Recurrent illness. Convalesces in Capri. Later visits and receives intermittent academic training in Rome, Florence, and Venice.

1906   To Paris. Early work influenced by Beardsley, Gauguin, Lautrec. Lives in Montmartre.

1908   Exhibits at *Salon des Indépendants*.

1909   Interest in sculpture encouraged by Brancusi. Ill, spends winter in Italy.

1910–13   Few paintings, concentrates on limestone sculptures. Chief patron is Dr. Paul Alexandre.

1914–15   Severe alcoholism, begins use of drugs. Meets Beatrice Hastings and Leopold Zborowski, who becomes his friend and dealer. First sales to dealer Paul Guillaume. Abandons sculpture.

1917   Meets Jeanne Hebuterne. One-man exhibition organized by Zborowski at Berthe Weill's.

1918–19   Tuberculosis aggravated by hashish and alcohol. Winter in Nice and Cagnes.

1920   Dies in Paris charity hospital, January 25.

MODIGLIANI AS SEEN BY
HIS FRIENDS

Ludwig Meidner: "Never before had I heard a painter speak of beauty with such fire. He showed me photographs of the work of early Florentine masters. Even more beautiful perhaps was what he had to say about them. Among more recent artists Toulouse-Lautrec and Gauguin fascinated him above all. But Modi was also interested in Whistler and his delicate tones."

Beatrice Hastings: "A complex character. A pig and a pearl. Met in 1914 at a *crémerie*. I sat opposite him. Hashish and brandy. Not at all impressed. Didn't know who he was. He looked ugly, ferocious, greedy. Met again at the Café Rotonde. He was shaved and charming. Raised his cap with a pretty gesture, blushed to his eyes, and asked me to come and see his work. Went. Always a book in his pocket. Lautréamont's *Maldoror.* First oil painting was of Kisling. Despised everyone but Picasso and Max Jacob. Loathed Cocteau. Never did any good work under drug."

Nina Hamnett: "He wore a black hat and a brown corduroy suit. He had curly black hair and brown eyes and was very good looking. He came straight up to me and said, pointing to his chest, 'Je suis Modigliani, Juif, Jew.' Unrolled his newspaper and produced some drawings. He said, 'Cinq francs.' They were very curious and interesting, long heads with pupil-less eyes."

Jean Cocteau: "Handsome, serious, romantic. He represented, perhaps, the last period of elegance in Montparnasse. I posed for three hours in Kisling's studio for both painters. Modigliani's portrait has since traveled a lot. It has also earned a fortune. At the time, however, we did not know that these sessions of posing, these drawings sketched at café terraces, these masterpieces at five francs, would not last forever."

Leopold Zborowski: "When he wasn't drunk, he could be a charming companion, laugh like a child, and be lyrical in translating Dante, making one love and understand him. He was naturally erudite, a good debater on art and philosophy, amiable and courteous. That was his real nature, but nevertheless he was just as often crazily irritable, sensitive, and annoyed for some reason he didn't know. When he was drunk, he was off his head."

André Salmon: "In some horrid retreat, lacking essentials, yet refusing to open the door to those who would have brought him necessities, he'd work as best he could in cold and hunger. He loathed professional models. He preferred the little *bonne* of Rosalie's restaurant, where fed masons, elderly Englishwomen, and a giant Swede who perched over his plate like the Tower of Pisa."

Lascano Tegui: "One night in January, 1920 was the last time I saw Modi alive. He was very drunk, his eyes were wild, and he was in one of his worst cantankerous moods, quarrelsome, abusive, and terribly emaciated. His friends wanted to take him home to the rue de la Grande Chaumière, where Jeanne Hebuterne awaited him anxiously. But, as usual, he wouldn't listen to anybody. When he was like that, nobody on earth could do anything with him, neither Zborowski nor even his fiancée."

SOME OTHER BOOKS
ABOUT MODIGLIANI

Maud Dale. *Modigliani.* New York: Knopf, 1929
Modigliani: Paintings, Drawings, Sculpture. New York: The Museum of Modern Art, 1951 (Illustrated catalog of an exhibition)
Arthur Pfannstiel. *Modigliani.* Paris: Seheur, 1929
André Salmon. *Modigliani, sa vie et son oeuvre.* Paris: Editions des Quatre Chemins, 1926

ACKNOWLEDGMENTS

In a book of art, it seems particularly fitting to acknowledge the work of craftsmen who contribute to its making. The color plates were made by Litho-Art, Inc., New York. The lithography is from the presses of The Meehan-Tooker Co., Inc., New York and the binding has been done by F. M. Charlton Co., New York. The paper was made by P. H. Glatfelter Co., Spring Grove, Pa. Our deepest indebtedness is to the museums, galleries, and private collectors who graciously permitted the reproduction of their paintings, drawings, and sculpture.